PREVIOUS BOOKS:

TRANSPARENCIES AND PROJECTIONS
(new rivers, 1969)

Halvard Johnson

The
Dance
of the
Red Swan

with etchings by
Kathy von Ertfelda

New Rivers Press, N.Y., 1971

Poems copyright © 1971 by Halvard Johnson
Etchings copyright © 1971 by Kathleen von Ertfelda
Library of Congress Catalog Card Number: 75-151101
ISBN 0-912284-15-3 (paper)
ISBN 0-912284-16-1 (cloth)
Book design by Marty Bernstein

Some of these poems first appeared in
STONY BROOK, POTPOURRI, DESPERADO, HEARSE,
TOLAR CREEK SYNDICATE, MONKS POND, SOU'WESTER,
QUETZAL, SUMAC, FRAGMENTS, CAFE SOLO, FOR NOW,
NEW: AMERICAN & CANADIAN POETRY, GNOSIS,
HANGING LOOSE, APPLE, CAYEY REVISTA,
and MANDALA.

This book was manufactured in the united states
for New Rivers Press, p.o. box 578, Cathedral
Station, New York, New York 10025 in first edition
of 700 copies (250 cloth, 450 paper)

for Keith & Heliose

contents

PART I

PART II

PART III

part 1

The Dance of the Red Swan

The pillows were white and fluffy,
an effect reminiscent of sitting in sidewalk cafes
on lower Fifth Avenue, back in the old days,
or of sipping Mexican Pernod with Irv and Harriet,
in their cabin high in the Sangre de Cristos.
The night outside would be cool and black with promise
of snow and the outhouse a good twenty steps from the back door.
But, in the old days, lower Fifth Avenue was peaceful,
even in wartime. The President had an apartment
in a building on Washington Square, but was never there
nowadays, according to the doorman, whom I never failed to ask.
All over the world, people were going to sleep and waking up,
fluffing their white pillows and going back to sleep again.

Irv and Harriet's cabin was actually in the Sacramentos,
the Sangre de Cristos being much farther north in New Mexico.
But there's something about Sangre de Cristo, the words,
in Spanish. There's also *arena*, which means sand. It can also mean
"arena", which is fair enough when the arena has sand in it.
But the names of things can fool you at times.
The Sangre de Cristos aren't in the least bit bloody
to the naked eye, and presidents' apartments don't always
have presidents in them. The Red Swan turns out to be
a woman in disguise. And north of the Sacramentos
and south of the Sangre de Cristos are the Sandias,
which are partly sand, but mostly rock.

As always

I have nothing to send you.
My bowels reek. It has been
raining here forever.
The news has been bad for weeks.
Even the neighbors have only petty
scandals to whisper about.
Birds of bright plumage
are reduced to rags,
dogs die and rot
in the gutters.
What did I do,
where are you?

A Cloud of Dust

This is in the valley of the Rio Grande.
You are standing in the hot sun
at the intersection of two roads — one
paved, a yellow line down the middle,
the other dirt, angling off through the cottonfields.

There is no one in sight. No birds in the sky.
You see the tracks made by cars and trucks turning
off of the dirt road and onto the paved one. You also see
those made by cars turning onto the dirt road,
but you cannot distinguish these from those made getting on.

And then there is a cloud of dust speeding up the valley
toward you. A cloud of dust moving with no wind.
And out of the dust cloud emerge six yellow buses
full of schoolchildren — Mexican, Indian, Anglo,
and mixtures of these. Schoolchildren, laughing

on their way to school. And then there is a seventh,
in which the children are no longer laughing. It stops
for you, and you enter.

Saga

*". . . caught in a strange country
for which no man would die."*
— *Philip Levine*

a strange rain falling
with its strange burden

1

and always running
legs heavy, chest heaving,
headful of memories, premonitions —

the tall rain
thrusting down through the dark, death-dealing

death riding the rays of the sun

2

thought of small rain, wind from the west,
sidewalks of cities in those days, shining,
slippery with light, those lost days

the big hand clasping my small one,
how warm it was there!

3

sunlight didn't matter: the heart
had its own darkness, as the sky
beyond blue is black

"Listen, my children, and you

16

the backyards were empty, everyone
moving away from the old block

     shall hear of the . . ."

     4

eyes are everywhere, like bits of broken glass,
watching the high tower for someone about to appear

& the watchers are being watched

     5

and the blind virgin
unravels herself
from the folds
of a flag

her body shining
in the falling rain

South Mountain

String quartets on Sunday afternoon.
Pittsfield, Massachusetts, nearby. Melville's Pittsfield!
From which in a car I followed a girl and her mother
all the way to New Haven, Connecticut.
After the concert, in a Howard Johnson's, they were eating
at a nearby table. The girl — nice legs,
nice breasts, nice face — she smiled at me,
her mother looked away. And I followed them
— didn't know if they knew it was me — all the way
to New Haven, their very front door.
How they sped through those small Connecticut towns
— got a ticket in one — surprised
as hell to see me in their rear-view mirror again
— the demon lover at their — her — heels.
The girl saw me pull up across the street,
smiled, said something to one of her two burly brothers,
who took one step and I was off for ever.

Anteroom

Under his chair, his hat
like a small, tired animal.
His hands resting on his knees.
A map of his life on his face.
Black angels whispering in his ears.

18

An Afternoon

A somber day. Hardly a bit of sun.
A woman with bare breasts. At intervals
there are cats, dancing in the high grass.
Clouds high overhead, not a solid gray.
Houses press in on all sides, none
of the doors or windows open. A widow,
solitary, sits behind her house, with bare
breasts, an invisible face, and no sun on it.

The notes of a song, picked out singly
on a piano. The hands mistaking. The eyes
moving among the objects presented to them.
Picking and choosing. Testing the qualities
of a certain kind of vision: single, flat,
unpenetrating. Things are so simple,
it seems to say. You never know, she says,
you hardly ever know. Once I was happy.

The day disintegrates into crashing chords
and discords, wild intervals of passionate
meditation. A touching of hands, and the faces
turn to each other. Lightning leaps
among the towering clouds. A gusty wind
springs up, wipes away a world.

Around about

Pushing aside
the thick branches,
branches thick with
tender & green leaves,
pushing aside the green
tender leaves, moving
into sunshine, looking
for, yellow sunshine
from blue sky,
sniffing a wet breeze,
pushing aside the thick
leaves, moving into
sunshine, looking for
berries?

Blue Railroad

Moving west along the canyon floor
scruffy mesquite & cottonwoods at river-edge,
likkered up like all the rest I saw
her high broad cheekbones ("her friends
call her La India, but not to her face")
dug her incongruous, powder-blue eyes
her "never-to-be-forgotten" smile.

River running faster now, down toward where
we came from, the desolate east. Who was it
said she would kill me? I forget now.
Bunch of stiffs in the next car maybe.
I said I'd gladly die. Those coppery thighs!
My moccasined, musky Rose of the West!

Higher up, the canyon walls pressing in
ominously, barely room for the tracks and a trickle
of water. Occasional points of light shining through
the blue darkness of the closing mountains. Before
it was complete, we had already come
to an understanding.

The Report

They stood across
the broad meadow from us,
their armor gleaming
in the sun, their horses
pawing the ground
and snorting.
At the sound of the trumpet
we charged them. Yells
and shouts filled the air.
They began to move toward us.
The field was filled
with a flurry of flags,
a clatter of weapons and armor,
a pounding of hooves and hearts.
As we reached their lines,
they broke, fell back
and melted
into the trees.
And before we knew it,
a gang of them
were throwing rocks at us
from the second floor
of Mr. Simpson's garage.
Luckily, most of us
had garbagecan tops
to use as shields.
But they
were throwing rocks!
And trying
to hit us, too!
Stevie Jackson got hit
in the head
and began to bleed

and cry. We started
to run away,
but another bunch
of them were hiding
in the Simpsons' garden.
Stevie got hit
by a stick
and fell down crying.
Jake Gibson, Fred
Martin, the lieutenant, and I
lobbed several grenades
into the densest part
of the foliage
where the bastards
were hiding. The radio
operator called in air support
before he got a bullet
in the gut. He screamed
for twenty minutes and then
died. The strike
was quick and clean,
leaving nothing
but charred jungle
in front of us.
Steve Jackson had a hole
between his eyes.
I threw him over my
shoulder and carried
him to the chopper.
We had been friends
all our lives.
The chopper lifted,
and those of us
who were left
fanned out

into the rain.
By the time I got home,
I was late for supper,
and Mother punished
me for getting wet.
Stevie Jackson spent
three weeks in the
hospital that time.

The Rider

carried herself well. Her mount,
while skirting the purple hill,
broke a leg, and, to its
everlasting credit
insisted on
finishing
the race
on three.

In the West

What do you do
out in the West
where the proud remnants
of European aristocracy
climb down from their phaetons
in haughty disarray
and walk, bare-headed, into the desert
never to be heard from again
unless it is in some dusty town
called Drygulch or Sidewinder,
bypassed by the railroad,
wells long ago gone dry,
where they take their parched throats,
their sun-cracked faces,
into the only saloon left in town
and ask the one-eyed barkeep
for champagne, and are told that
there's one bottle left
which he's kept for just
such an occasion?

Weekend

It was late Saturday afternoon.
By the time she got home
from the motel, she was
already desperate.

Museum Piece

Introduc— tion	He lived his life as though it were a work of art, surrounded though he was by piano students turned bankers.
I. A Touch of Magic	His cup of tea was paradox and conundrum. His lively mind thriving on contradiction, infesting it with its own inextricable logic.
A. The Nec- essary Nude	Accosting voluptuous young ladies, requesting them to divest themselves in the face of Historical Necessity and the deplorable Social Graces.
B. Shaking the Pillows of Tradition- al Esthetes	All of this had a numbing effect, giving way to an unlikely series of series, the legendary plumbing, the plumbing was numbing, the shovels were digging, ideas taking root, another round of interminable conundrumming coming to an end.
C. With Mild Abandon	Then — ah, then — to give it all up to upchuck it all up, all up, chuck it all up, up all, chuck it up.
II. The Mid- section	His early period laid a firm foundation for his middle years (sometimes known as the Diddle Years) in which he did
A. Liddle or Nudding	liddle or nudding. Noodling around in his Attic studio, cracking valises, playing chest, smoking reflections or pipestems, punishing his friends. And his friends
B. Sticks & Stones	(if *you* can call them so, for I, *I* never shall) his friends came always slinking by to see

26

if there was anything new to be catalogued.
And would look him from toe to head in contempt,
call him an aging terrible infant
and slinking slink away.

III. The Face of Adversity	The end of the so-called Second World War found him somewhere in Central Europe, wandering in a daze in his self-styled garden, thinking
A. Anton	of his good friend Anton, whom he hadn't seen since that summer in Munich before the war,
B. His Wish	and devoutly wishing that some drunken American soldier would come by and put a bullet in his *cabeza*.
IV. The Final Showing	A landscape full of twigs, dirty leaves, and autumnal splendor. A glowing amber lamp held aloft by the left hand of a three-dimensional nude, golden curls lapsing onto her shoulder. Her lovely legs are spread provocatively before a shimmering waterfall and a small pond.
Epilogue	He died as he would have wanted to.

He

walks down
one side of the
street instead
of the other for
some clear reason
speaks kindly of
those who are
dead or have more
money than he
has always stops
to pat stray dogs
on their heads wears
pants to bed so as
not to offend
the ladies

To Barbados

What we were never aware of was
that Mary & Jane had run off to Barbados
where they are living together
as husband and wife
we hope they will always be happy
we were also unaware
that a first cousin of Mary's
on her mother's side of the family
has been confined to an asylum
for most of her natural life
& that Jane's father's uncle
was a self-made millionaire
who died in poverty on the third day
of the seventh month of his eightieth year
he did not rise again insofar as is known
we are sure that Jane's family
wouldn't have stood for it
Mary's family also pretended to gentility
after the elopement an aunt of hers was heard
to ask why she had to do it with a Baptist

On a Lexington Avenue Bus

You fall in love bit by bit,
piece by piece. First,
her legs, sleek and nylony,
cutting along E. 47th St.
Then a quarter profile
from the back of the crowd
at the bus stop. The back of
her neck, a wisp or two of hair,
as she pauses at the fare-box.

Day by day you inch up on her
in the bus. A glimpse of
her smile drives you crazy. You catch
a whiff of her perfume and the next day
you rub elbows with her. The bus
lurches to a stop. You feel her breast on
the back of your arm. This is Friday,
naturally, so you have the weekend
to think about it.

Monday, you make your move. You brush
her buttocks with your hand. Next,
a day or two later, you let her know
she is definitely being felt. A squeeze,
a goose. The weeks are passing like days.
She hasn't called a cop. You slowly turn
her around, look into her eyes. She looks
feelingly into yours. Days pass like weeks.
She lifts one of your hands to her breast.

Soon enough your other hand is at her crotch,
feeling around. Her thighs are gripping it
like a vise. Working it around. Her eyes

have been closed for weeks now. Her breast
heaving. She's gasping for breath. She's
ripping your shirt with her nails.
And when it's all over,
she slowly opens her eyes. Her hot eyes.
"You're wonderful, you're wonderful!" she sighs.

You want to know her name.
Where she lives. Who she is.
What she's doing this weekend.
She puts a finger to your lips.
"You're wonderful," she breathes.
Her finger taps your teeth.
"You were wonderful, dear,
but don't say a word.
Let's not spoil it."

On the Streets

They are waiting
their toes are
curling in their
shoes they don't
make any sound
but I know they
are waiting there
their eyes are
narrow slits and
their hands are not
in their pockets
they are waiting
behind doors or
in alleys I can
hear their breathing
if I hold my
breath

The Return of the Queen

Her departure
had been the occasion
of general consternation.

Several committees were formed
to seek ways and means of bringing
her back. These were called Ways & Means
Committee # 1, Ways & Means Committee # 2, Ways
& Means Committee # 3, and so on.

These committees would meet early in the morning,
before the sun rose so high that their members would
be unable to think very clearly, what with the heat and all.

Most committees found it advisable to divide themselves into
sub-committees: as, Ways & Means Committee # 42, Sub-Committee
A, Sub-Committee B, and so on. The sub-committees would usually
meet in the evening on a more informal basis,
often in a neighborhood bar & grill.

Mornings, the sub-committees would report back
to their respective committees, which would then consider
the merits of their recommendations, separate the wheat
from the chaff, as it were, and send the wheat
along to the Central Committee,
made up of committee chairmen
and chaired by the King.

The Central Committee met once a week (but only on Tuesday
afternoons, so as not to interfere with the King's golf schedule).
It would discuss the proposals of the various committees
and invariably decide that none of them were workable.
Each chairman would defend the suggestions

of his own committee and attack
all the others.

The upshot, of course, was that the King grew more and more furious
by the week. He was put off his game and developed an almost
incurable slice. In a rage, he asked his caddy what he should do.

Send someone to ask her to return, the caddy said.
The King sent the caddy. The Queen returned.
To universal applause.

Moral: If a system works, don't knock it.

The Projects

They insist always
that we leave off this
for that, they feel,
it seems, as though
continuity isn't everything,
isn't anything, in fact,
much worth considering

As we must, we take them
at their word, jettisoning
project after project,
rarely, if ever, bringing
anything to completion,
always moving on from
one thing to the next

We plant, but neither weed
nor harvest, we put up houses
and leave them without roofs, we end
our bridges half-way across the

Variables

There were other ways.
It might have been done at night,
      it might never have been done at all.
         Someone was always turning
pages, making rattling sounds
in the next room.
         The variations were endless,
and these are only some of them:

/unsolved problems/
the semblance of reality, fractioning
of time & space
        "Let those who do not understand
have simultaneous translation"

/premonitions/
q. how fast is the Crab Nebula expanding?
a. 1000 miles per second
q. how far is it now?
a. I don't know

(Some details have been omitted in order
to show the precise nature of the problem.)

/reverberations/
q. how slowly is the Crab Nebula expanding?
a. 1000 miles per second
q. how would you define a "second"?
a. as the time it takes the Crab Nebula
   to swallow up another thousand miles
   of interstellar space

/definitions/
q. reality?
a. what is real, or seems to be real,
   also, under certain circumstances, what is unreal
q. life?
a. amino acids & nucleotides watered every second day
q. Crab Nebula?
a. greedy space-eater

The pages are always being turned.
There is always someone in the next room turning pages.
There is a wind
blowing across his desk
from an open window.

No Chance

Our guide and our bearers have fled.
The snowfields are blazing.
At this altitude, the sky is almost black.

We have attempted the South Face and failed.
The storm broke our descent.

Our fingers are frozen.

The world is white and then black
and then white again.

We had no chance for the top.

Cheer

Your unfortunate situation
reminds me of a time I was alone
in a strange city. It was a dark
and obscure day, as though I had
brought my own weather.

Some friends of mine
were to have met me at the station,
but seemed to have forgotten all about me.
So I was obliged to walk.

My friends, evidently, had moved to another city.
For three days I tried one address after another,
climbing stairways, knocking at doors.
Three nights I slept in a park.

You are not alone you see. Like you,
I suffer, thrill at the thought of it.

Losses

Someone he knew
was speaking to him
from very far away, so far
he could barely see him.

They were sitting at an oblong table
and he was at the other end of it.
He could see his lips move
but could not hear what
he was saying.

He had been told that he would know him,
but now that they were face to face
he wasn't sure he remembered.
Blue eyes and sandy hair.
He couldn't be over thirty-five.

The table was round now,
and he seemed to be screaming at him.
He could almost remember where it had been,
where he had met him. His blue eyes.
Why was he screaming?
His sandy hair.

Maker of Devils

"Your self-delusions exact
their own price
in their own time."

His own last words,
from the fire.

A fantastic life!
A man depraved by vice,
as they thought. Refined.
Perverse.

Unknown to those
living in his own house.
Spied upon. Whispered about.

There was too much rain & then
there was not enough. Floods
followed by drought. His
magic was strong.

When the crops had failed
and they were hungry,
proverbs, folklore,
and even astrology
proved small consolation.

He makes devils, they said.
He speaks with the dead.
He eats the unborn.

part 2

Nothing from Nothing

 Night falls heavily through the trees,
the wet ground holds it.
In the morning, there will be fresh tracks
in the wet ground. And no one will know
who left them there.
The night is dismal
and we are afraid of it.
Morning dawns grayly, and there are
things that have happened that we
know nothing about.

A man's life is like — well, what?
The moisture found on early morning grass
has fallen silently during the night
and vanishes before noon.
There is the sudden thrashing of an animal
in the high grasses and reeds
at the edge of a scum-covered lake.

The smile of a woman so beautiful
that she is confined to a garden
with walls so high that no one
can see her, with walls so high
that no one can see her smile.

A beautiful afternoon. The trellises were disarranged.
The palace eunuchs were trepanning the Emperor
in his very own garden. The power struggle
appalled all of us who knew of it. We few.

Nothing from nothing. From nothing comes nothing.
Nothing comes to nothing. Nothing added to nothing gives you nothing.
If you have nothing and nothing is taken away, you are left with
nothing, nothing less than you had to begin with. Nothing from
nothing. Nothing more, nothing less.

Consent to Die

My power is very great against you. My dreams
have been auspicious for weeks now. My arm
throbs with strength. My heart pounds strongly
in pursuit of you. Your name is weak, is weak.

All signs are favorable to your death. Your death star
is in the proper quarter. Your life star sinks
into the sea. A tree bent away from you as you passed.
Your wife and children were seen moving away from you at the same time.

Consider my need for your houses, your goods.
My land cries out to be added to yours. The eyes of your wife
seek mine. I said your name to the wind, and the wind took it away
and hurled it down upon the rocks. And the waters covered it.

Song

Walking where water
never flows and I
had heard that you
and I were never yet
wherever she was singing
or would sing a stone
that's under water when
her flower went awry
a song her sister knows
or sometimes said she knew

Flung Roses

Beneath the bough —
O, melancholy devil
    O, sonofabitch
I'd like to rip your clothes off
See you walk naked among the rose petals

My Green Office

The mountains around Cayey are green.
The walls of my office are green.
Dark green at the bottom. Light green toward the top.
My office is on the second floor of a white building.
The building is one of several white buildings
arranged in a semi-circle, at the center of which
are two flag poles, flying the flags of Puerto Rico
and the United States.
My office has only one window.
Until two years ago the buildings and grounds were
a U.S. Army base known as Henry Barracks.
Old Army men still think of this place as Henry Barracks.
The parade ground is now used for track and field events,
although an R.O.T.C. unit marches there from time to time.
From the window of my green office
I can look across the green campus
and see the green mountains.
There was a sign upstairs, over the urinals.
"Don't throw butts in the urinals," it said,
"and we won't piss in your buttcans."
This sign was taken down.
From my window I can watch the students
walking across the green campus.
The students can look up and see me watching them.
They cannot see me when I am sitting at my desk
or standing well away from the window.
The mural depicting the Last Supper
in what was once the mess hall
and is now the snack bar
was also taken down.
My office has only one door.
It is directly opposite the window.

Just above the door, the word EXIT is painted
in red letters three inches high.
Just outside the back door of the snack bar
is a small sign that says MESS HALL.
Some things here have not been changed.

The Invasion

I am sitting on my porch reading.
Across the street is the city welfare office,
a woman in red is sweeping the sidewalk.
Down the street to my right is the municipal hospital.
People come and go. A Catholic high school
at the end of the street. The girls in their white
blouses and blue jumpers pass beneath me.
To my left, a group of men playing dominoes,
with loud exclamations in Spanish.
Somewhere, off in the distance, the Russians
are madly marching on Finland.

Centers of Gravity

Last night,
the summer
wasn't very
warm, I slept
with mother,
my hand
on her fat
breast.

Sometimes
I wake
up and feel
things
crawling
on me.

I always
think
of that
soldier
leading
a chicken
on a string.

A Field of Yellow Flowers

I am walking through a field
of yellow flowers. Under a tree
in the middle of the field of yellow
flowers sits an Arab in a white burnoose.
From the middle of the field of yellow flowers
my Arab stares at me, advancing toward him
through a field of yellow flowers.

How I Lost You

We were picking our way among bits
and pieces of debris. I stopped to listen.
Behind a large rock, a bird was singing.
By the time it was finished, you had moved out of sight.

Time & Place

Time and again, I watched her
go up to the door
             & return,
without having entered.
                    The spring breeze
stirring in the garden, ruffling
the curtains of her bed.

The curling smoke of our cigarettes
flattening out near the ceiling.
Our ambiguous conversations,
returning always to the same themes
: mockeries, self-parodies.

          The fading sunlight,
          the other side of the door.

Sanderson's Glance

Sanderson's glance fell on me.
One of his eyes was bigger than the other.

Do you know my name? he said.
His nose was like a big, red strawberry.

Sanderson, I said.
His face was leaning, trying to smile.

You're right, young man.
Sanderson is me.

Early Mornings

Reminding me of the beginnings of things —

    long journeys, early breakfast with the lights
    on in the kitchen, pulling out of the driveway
    just before daybreak, a thermos of hot coffee
    in the glove compartment, my father yawning
    as we drove away

    the first day of my life, the first day
    of the world, moving out of the shadow, the whirl
    of forms, slow spinning of planets and galaxies

    the first damn girl I was old enough to think
    I was in love with, a smile as bright as the sun,
    but before that a shoulder as cold as the depths of space,
    gradual warming after chill

    our man and machinery poised at their border, the sun coming up
    behind us, we could see them beneath us, moving around
    in the shadow, we hit them as the sun hit their eyes

Flood

How desperately
the coffee-colored river
surged through the streets,
the town you had abandoned.

Lost

Hazy horizons. The sky
that never stops turning.
She is lost.
Wandering in circles
in the cane-brakes
by the river,
where no one will find her.
She doesn't notice
the birds turning
in the air above her
& the sky above
their turning, turning.

The Burning of Cities

The flat, blue light is below us.
Your hands move shamelessly
on my back & thighs.
Trees emerge from a velvet background.
Move this way & that. Something is
moving between them, among them.
You are lovely, but what
are you saying? The words
make no sense to me.

The light is leaving. The bay & the mountains
behind it will soon be engulfed by darkness.
It is warm, the water now, lapping at our feet.
But what cities, what fires, do you mean?

Leaves

delicadas,
            green, tracing
into, under, through
beyond green

                    fire,
green consuming mountains
corrosive, consuming

it was green, she
                said
            turning a pale hand

Girl on a Horse

Oh, the richness of it:
the dark horse scampering
through the sea-breaks,
gulls crying overhead,
the way she turned her head
toward us, smiling her dark smile.
A wave of her hand and she was off
again, down the beach, turning
and galloping back, smiling,
smiling. And the animal beneath her,
glistening and snorting,
snorting and glistening.

Alborada

Trees opening,
flowers with no eyes,
a long dawning, morning words
turn Barbara's way, hear
mountains wish,
                    blonde stranger
conversation piece
                    of the sun world

Last Light

Up the coast you know
San Pedro and the rest
of those small towns.
Not much rain, but you
could hear violins on hot
summer evenings, surf
curling toward the beach.
And if you'd ever thought
to leave your hotel room,
walk the cooling sand, you'd
have seen a kneeling girl
picking out bits of red coral
the last tide left among
the seaweed and palm fronds
at the water line. Hearing
your step, she'd look up.
Seeing you, the last light
on your face, she would have
smiled, though she did not know you.
And, in the darkness closing in, her smile
might have saved you.

Seascape

We are surrounded
by the sea, the sea
is all around us.
We are ourselves
in the circles of the sea,
ourselves to the end
of the curving sun and sea.
Today is a windy day,
we are so happy.
We are ourselves in
the circles, ourselves
to the ends of the sea.
No wind today,
and we are happy.
We are ourselves in
the sand, the circling sun,
the curling sea, the curving
ends of what we barely see.

Las Montañas Verdes

from the shade,
the shade of the brim
            of his hat
they move,
a yellow car turning into a narrow street
from the shade of a tree among trees

turning into,
what should we call it,
this avenue of fading yellow trees

it was not as though nothing had happened
: there were his eyes, following us
moving like leaves, through the chromatic forest

**

& his women, moving in twos through the town,
along the thin sidewalks, on their heavy legs

& his daughters, with lighter hearts & heads,
sitting, mornings, within his walled gardens
as though nothing had happened

**

& their green mountains, ringing the town,
dreaming of yellow cars cruising the highways
as they have for centuries

from The Letters

             Begin with an apology,
1)   some reason for not having written
             for seven months
                           one month in a hospital,
             six in the mountains, convalescing

                 continue with something
             relatively unimportant,
             like the weather —

                    the dry air,
             with brief showers in the afternoon,
             the patterns of clouds on the hillside

                 the way the sun shines
                 through the broad, green banana leaves

             tell her how those tiny lizards breathe,
             those tiny balloons in their throats

             Oh, God!   The pain of it.
2)   Why haven't I seen you
             in all these weeks?

             What was it?

             I didn't mean to force myself on you,
             I thought you . . . I wanted . . . I . . .

             Not that.
3)   No.

I've never seen so brilliant a green
as in those banana leaves with the sun behind them,
the veins in them standing out
like . . .

What was it?
I thought everything was going well with us,
that we wanted the same things for ourselves.

No, a letter like that it's better to write
4)   and throw away.

Tell her about ugly things,
those people we read about in the paper,
the foaling mare, clubbing it to death,
tying a rope to the foal,
dragging it out, killing it

A strange mood.
5)   Nobody around now.

I'm sitting on the veranda, wishing I had
some cigarettes. Occasionally, I can bribe
one of the chambermaids into buying some
when she's in town.

She smuggles them in past the doctors, the guards,
sweet girl — she returns my letters unopened

The least she could do would be read them,
don't you think?

Tell me something about yourself.

6) What do you hope for?
Do they beat you very often there? Is your condition
incurable? Are they treating you well?

Things are very difficult here.

7) The man in the next cell is out of his mind.
He keeps writing imaginary letters
to imaginary people, usually ex-wives
or girlfriends.
Because I'm a writer, he always asks me
to help, check his spelling, etc.
I think of you always,
you and the children.
They're beating the horses again.
Down in the cellar. In the dark.
I love you and miss you.
Why don't you ever write?
The sun is warm.
It's been months now.
Why don't you write?

Nets

1

Among her belongings
were found three pieces of coral,
probably collected on her trip to Tahiti.
A spider was living in one of the pieces of coral.

She knew she was dying
when they wheeled her into the terminal ward

& she refused to admit visitors.

2

She knew she was dying the day she was born.
Not an obsession, it was, with her, an acknowledged fact.

But she seemed to be obsessed by nets. Nets & webs. Her talk
and her writing were full of them. In her apartment,
the cobwebs were never disturbed.

The last time I visited her, she entrusted her diary
to my keeping and told me where I could find it.

This is one of the last entries, dated 8 August, 1965:

3

They are traps. I have always loved them,
but they are traps. Since that day on the beach,
the water placid behind the reef, I have known
I would not be one of the ones who escaped
or were thrown back. I would be hauled to the beach

to do my flip-flop of death on the dry sand.
Pray God that mine will be one of those that command
the eye with their vigor and beauty.

4

She died in her sleep and was found in the morning.
Someone said she was beautiful

The Music

How much escapes us, in respect
of ourselves moving with
and away from each other.
Carrying souvenirs, each
to the other. Bits of dead skin
beneath our nails. Loose hair
on our shoulders. The tune of a song
we've forgotten the words to. The words
we can't remember how to sing.

At Sundown

Under a black tree
at the edge of the cliff
something was turning
the day to its good end

and his worries
left off where the water began,
the edge of that world
we most fear falling into.

Among other things he heard her voice
calling to him, singing for him
behind him, among the dark trees —
the water shining before him.

The Difference

then someday someone
will knock on
your door, having
walked for centuries
to get where you are

having been offered
a chair, he will take
off his coat
and sit down, smiling
though tired

you will offer him a drink & he will refuse, politely
there will be an uncomfortable silence, as though
not knowing where to begin

        at last, you will speak
        you will clear your throat
        & ask him where he has come from
        but what you really want to know
        is what he has come for

      & you've begun to suspect
      when he turns to you and says
      'Let's speak of that in the morning'

and in the morning, of course, you rise to find
that he has already left

        and it is almost evening
        before you begin

     to notice the difference

part 3

Landscape with Yellow Birds

I

This is what I believe:

Below the visible surface of the world
is an immense, brilliantly lighted room.
Throughout the room are millions
and millions of pictures, each
a representation of the world upstairs.

II

Mine would be a landscape with yellow birds,
surrounded by fantastic vegetation. It would be night,
and the birds would not be flying. There would be
a moon. A full moon transfiguring the green
and yellow jungle.

III

Many complain that five of my six yellow birds
are upside-down, and that the strange plant-life
seems to be rooted in the sky.

The truth, my friend, is that you, the viewer,
are upside-down, and only one
of my six yellow birds.

From a Window

Standing here at this upper window
I see two men shouting at each other
in the distance. The sun behind me
flashes on a knife before me, and I see
one fall, collapse and die, and hear
what must have been a scream.

The Songs of the Eastern Mountains

Forever bringing us sorrow,
coming across the smooth lake to us
in a gray haze.
                        Coming across the smooth
water to us, across the waving grass.

The voices of women reaching us
through the smoke of their fires,
the vapors rising from the surface of the lake.

They are singing our death songs. They call us
by our names. And the men there are sharpening knives
and putting on armor.

When they are ready to fight, and the singing has ended,
disaster for us begins.

At the Edge

Wondering if I would ever see you again
I walked to the edge of town and sat down
in the darkness wondering if I would ever
hear the sound of your voice telling me
that you loved me so much that you would
do almost anything in the world for me
except walk through that town in darkness
and by yourself for the several moments
it would take me to reach you to reach
out to you in the darkness from where I was
sitting all by myself at the edge of town
wondering if I could ever touch you again.

Drift

Outdistancing the others
we came to a small, deserted island —

> a curving beach of white sand,
> a fringe of palm trees heaving in the wind

II

We were depressed by the heavy smell of death in the air.
I spent half of the night looking for you.   You, traipsing
around, the hem of your dress
trailing in the water.

III

And from the air,
drifting in on the trade winds,
we see below us the giants
hunched over beneath the clear, blue-green water.

They are waiting, biding their time.
Only the tops of their heads break the surface.

What I Want

I want those first words desperately trailing
off through the underbrush, spattering light
on the wall of my cave, mumbling along
like her tiny feet in the carpeted hallway.
I want our transitions as smooth as cream,
elegant as our hands upon satin, clear
as cold water running over polished stones,
as a hand and a hand on a silken knee.
Our lives should be no longer than our arms
bearing arms through the soft, fleshy night,
stretching, reaching out softly from our sides
in cadenced light to a tentative ending.
And the last two, like the first, in tandem,
hand in hand, and screaming to the end.

The Extra-Inning Ballgame

Wanting things to go on forever,
yet craving the apocalypse.
Reading the last few pages at one word a minute.
Wanting to teeter forever at the brink of the abyss,
and loving every minute of it.

The solid single lashed over second.
A shortstop's arm, just long enough to catch it.

Smash

What we need
is to examine this from as many
viewpoints as possible

There, for example, is an old woman pulling on her hose.
She has rolled down the tops of them, pointed her toes into them,
and begun to pull them up over her calves, her knees, her thighs.
She smoothes them to her bulging flesh and then with a few tugs
hitches them to her corset by means of the straps depending therefrom.
She turns her back on a floor-length mirror, and twisting around as far
as she can examines and adjusts the straightness of her seams.

And then, in broad daylight, she turns and walks away.

Circles

It's my fault.
There are circles within circles within circles.
They are like ripples on the surface
of a perfectly round pond
when a perfectly round pebble
is dropped straight down into it
precisely at its center.

They just keep spreading, getting wider and wider,
and even at the water's edge the impulse continues,
diminishing with each successive ripple,
but making themselves felt nonetheless
as they go on spreading wider and wider,
more and more minutely, world without end.

I know it's my fault. But all those others
only stand around in a circle, wringing their hands
and crying. Tears springing to their round eyes,
almost as though they were not enjoying themselves
at my humiliation. They cry for all of us, they say,
they cry for us all. They range in a circle around me.
Their tongues are tiny dots in the circles of their mouths.

Sunlight Imposes
(after a line by Jack Collom)

Several times a day I go outside & peek at the sun.
It is always the same: Between 8 & 4, just a bunch
of colored disks — red, yellow, green, blue — popping out
at you POP POP POP POP. Just like that.

After four o'clock in the afternoon it always gets bigger
& bigger and redder & redder, until, like the swollen
nose of a wino, it slips below the bar.

Sometimes at night I go outside and look at the moon,
catching sunlight on the rebound as it were. But when
the moon is full, on the far side of earth, I think
of myself on the moon, watching the sun in the dark of the earth.

Blend

Sea-swimming the mastertank
the brainwaves spilling over us like something
I would rather not talk about
                      her face
though there was nothing particularly wrong or right
with it did it seem unusual that she did not return
with us that no one ever seemed to hear from her
again.
      It was the same old story   It was his wife
who wouldn't listen to him his protestations   He
spoke to her of love
                & every bit of her attention
    went right out the window, whistling Dixie

I should have thought that that would be enough to warn
you. But, tell me, now that you know:
Do you have any sincere regrets?

Moving. The Air.

Specialties of light.
Among the mountains, voices to be heard.
The clean air, to be seen, looked into.

The campers in Dog Canyon were not surprised.
Perpendicular walls shut out the sun.
And yet — the air was light,
light & air, moving.
                    The mountains themselves
seemed to move with it, breathing.

Moving air, carrying with it the smoke of campfires.
In early morning, the smells of bacon and coffee,
swirling through the trees.
The trees themselves: aspen, pine, and spruce.

Three hours of sun between the walls, an afternoon
of drowsy breathing. Sweet smell of horses.

After dark, distant sounds have an edge of fear.
And the chill in the air smells like ice.
Ice moving down the mountains again.
Down from the top of the earth.

Late, after midnight, between midnight & dawn,
our eyes turn out into space. The frozen stars,
suspended in nothingness. The one time of day
we can see where we're going.